LOVE JOURNEY

A 31-DAY JOURNEY TO FINDING THE LOVE YOU HAVE FOR YOURSELF

EBONY N'TANTALA

PUBLISHED BY VALUABLE U PUBLISHING

EBONY N'TANTALA

Copyright © 2023 Ebony N'Tantala

All rights reserved.

No part of this book may be reproduced or stored in a retrieval system, or transmitted in any form or by any means, electronic, mechanical, photocopying, recording, or otherwise without express written permission of the publisher.

Cover Design By: Ebony N'tantala

ISBN: **9798499435342**

DEDICATION

To my Awesome Amazing 4. My four heartbeats.
Tre, you finding us was an answer to my prayers.
You all were my reason for living before I realized
I had to live to show you all how amazing each one
of you are. I am grateful God allowed me to be
y'alls mother. It's been a crazy ride but
I wouldn't change it for the world.
I love you all.

EBONY N'TANTALA

CONTENTS

	ACKNOWLEDGEMENTS	viii
1	Put Your Oxygen on First	3
2	Realizing you're Loved	20
3	Who are You	33
4	Yesterday is Gone	41
5	You're an Individual	51
6	You're Not Alone	60
7	It's okay to say NO	69
8	Uplift Someone in Need	78
9	Poetry in Motion	87
10	We All Need Correction	95
11	Consult the Chief Consultant	102
12	Healing & Deliverance	109
13	ME, DAY!!!	117
14	Who's Your Crew?	128
15	The Measure of it All	134
16	Knowing Your Heart's Desire	142
17	Don't Keep Secrets	150
18	Write your Vision	160

19	Punch Fear in the Face	166
20	Come out of the Cave	177
21	Let it all go	183
22	Stop it Already	189
23	Speak Life	196
24	Open your Heart	203
25	Moving Forward	209
26	Christ isn't Going Anywhere	215
27	You're powerful; Stand Out	223
28	Don't just sit there	229
29	Take out the Trash	237
30	Speak up, So they can hear you in the Back	243
31	Fresh Start	251
32	What the Bible Says about Love	257

LOVE JOURNEY

Acknowledgment

I thank God for loving me so much that he constantly puts up with me and my shenanigans. For loving me unconditionally and showing me what I look like through His eyes.

I thank my momma, she never allowed me to quit and has forever been in my corner.

I thank my dad for making sure I remember I am working towards what God has for me.

I thank The Edinburg Ignitors, You ladies rock, thanks for the love and the prayers. To my team at Valuable University and Sips & Sunsets, You all are amazing.

LOVE JOURNEY

EBONY N'TANTALA

LOVE JOURNEY

A 31-DAY JOURNEY ON FINDING AND LOVING WHO YOU ARE.

Unless otherwise noted, The English Standard Bible was used for bible verses.

EBONY N'TANTALA

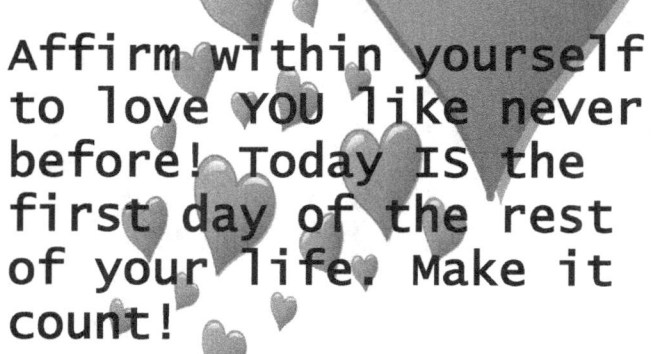

Affirm within yourself to love YOU like never before! Today IS the first day of the rest of your life. Make it count!

LOVE JOURNEY

LOVE JOURNEY

Matthew 7:3-5

Why do you see the speck
that is in your brother's eye,
but do not notice the log that
is in your own eye?
Or how can you
say to your brother, 'Let me take
the speck out of your eye,'
when there is the log in
your own eye? You hypocrite,
first take the log out of your own eye,
and then you will see clearly
to take the speck
out of your brother's eye.

Chapter 1
Put Your Oxygen on First

Why can we see what everyone else needs to improve their lives? We happily celebrate them and acknowledge their worth. But when it comes to our lives, we tend to be blinded by the negativity we see within ourselves. Projecting the anger and hurt we have within ourselves onto others, becoming rude, mean, and sometimes downright nasty. By refusing to acknowledge or recognize our accomplishments, we are saying, to those around us,

"I don't want to make you feel inferior, so I will make myself feel that way instead." But is that our actual reasoning? Or is that our way of telling ourselves it's okay not to recognize the greatness within us?

Loving you means you making yourself a priority! You still look out for your responsibilities; you make yourself your first responsibility so that you can deal with your other obligations more readily.

Prioritizing all of those around you and not yourself is not responsible or healthy. To truly love, we must first learn to take time to care for ourselves unapologetically. Why? Because you matter!

Trying to help or save others before we are willing to help or protect ourselves is like putting on someone else's oxygen before our own. What we are doing is slowly dying in our rescue attempt, and we are not helping them to our fullest capacity or capabilities. Think about it, if you die while putting on someone else's oxygen before you apply your own, what good are you to them?

Putting our oxygen on first makes us more clear-headed to assist those looking to us for help safely. With oxygen (self-Love) coursing through our brains, we can clearly see what those surrounding us need.

EBONY N'TANTALA

One of the first steps to becoming an influential person and a person who can genuinely love others is to truly love yourself.

Journal Time

Self-assessment

Respond to each question by writing your answers in your journal.

1. When you spend time alone, how do you feel?
   a. I'm fine. I like spending time alone.
   b. I don't try to be alone. I'm more comfortable around other people.
   c. Sometimes I'm okay alone; other times, I want to be around others.

2. Do you take time to encourage yourself like

you encourage other people?
a. Yes, I'm my best cheerleader.
b. No, I'm better at advising others than following the advice I give.

3. What's your favorite color?

4. What's your favorite time of year?

5. Do you allow people to compliment you?
   -If you allow people to compliment you, do you receive the compliment or blow it off like it's no big deal?

6. How do you like your hair?

7. Name at least three things you love about yourself in each category?
   a. Physically
   b. Emotionally
   c. Spiritually
   d. Mentally

8. Do you love yourself when you "fail" as much as you do when you succeed?

I promise I am not having you ask yourself these questions to torture you. You must know who you are and love yourself for who you are. I want you to understand why you do not feel worthy enough to be loved as much as you love someone else. I want you to look at yourself and see how amazing and incredible you are in the eyes of God. You are a beautiful work of art.

You must also realize that no one is absolutely and utterly happy with who they are or how they look. There will always be something you can do better. Whether or not you like all of you, loving yourself is a must. No one in this world is perfect, but

God has made you fearfully and wonderfully.

If you had difficulty answering these questions, I believe it's time for you to get to know yourself better.

So commit, right now, to use your journal and witness your progress as you continue on your love journey.

EBONY N'TANTALA

Love Journey #1

I'm striving to be seen as one who truly loves.

Not the fake church love that one speaks while in the four walls of "the building" where they believe God dwells.

No, I'm talking about a love that shows the love of the God I serve.

Letting others see He dwells within the building of me.

walls down, barriers destroyed, fences removed type of love.

Flowing freely from within me to the multitude around me type of love. As the Body of Christ, we need to check our love level.

The Body has become so comfortable with our "Christianese" ways and false religious talk that we don't genuinely know how to love. We become so used to performing for a crowd of folks who may or may not believe in the God we serve. We have become so self-absorbed we fight one another for honors and titles, forgetting God loves each one of us.

We get so wrapped up in titles and name-dropping that we've forgotten the Name that matters most. The Name above all names, the Name that every knee shall bow to and every tongue shall confess to Jesus: Yeshua, the Messiah, The Lily of the Valley, Logos, The Son of God.

So many have become enamored with presenting others with the "knowledge" they've acquired, ignorantly allowing compassion to fall by the wayside!
Willfully allowing arrogance and pride to flourish in its place.

The true meaning of Love has become forgotten.
Instead, it has become a tool many use to enslave the desperate and needy.

EBONY N'TANTALA

Stop allowing words that you don't mean in your heart to fall from your lips.

Love you the way you want to be loved.

Romans 8:38-39

For I am sure that neither

death nor life, nor angels

nor rulers, nor things present

nor things to come,

nor powers, nor height

nor depth, nor anything else in all creation,

will be able to separate us

from the love of God in

Christ Jesus our Lord.

EBONY N'TANTALA

Chapter 2
Realizing you are loved.

What is love? What does it mean to be loved? How should I love? Who should I love? Am I loved? Why doesn't anyone love me? Are these questions you've asked yourself, God, your mom, or your best friend? Have you been searching for love and coming up short or empty-handed? Do you feel you love people more than they love you? If you answered yes to any of these questions, you might suffer from a lack of loving yourself.

When we are unable to love ourselves, we tend to project the negative feelings we have for ourselves onto other people. We see them how we see ourselves and have a negative view and outlook on life in general.

Some people try to overcompensate for the negative feelings they have for themselves by helping everyone and anyone out. Because this is the way they have validation and feel valued.

Neither of these situations is healthy for either party. Often, this happens because we don't feel loved, needed, or wanted. Often we cannot love others properly because we haven't learned to love ourselves properly or no one taught us how to love ourselves the right way.

First, we need to establish that you are truly loved and wanted. John 3:16 states, "For God <u>so</u>, loved the world, that He gave His

ONLY begotten Son, that whosoever believes in him shall not perish but have everlasting life."

My friend, you are in this world and a "whosoever." Praise God! God loves you; Jesus loves you. Christ could've come off that cross at any time. He could've said, "Pops, I don't want to do this; these people aren't worth it." But He didn't. He allowed Himself to be bruised, battered, and broken for you. He hung on that cross to make sure you would know that you are loved, and you would have a choice to accept His love and everlasting life.

Are there going to be times that you feel you don't matter? Or that you're alone, stressed, and bogged down, life altogether overwhelming? Yes! But that does not mean that God does not love you or that Christ isn't interceding on your behalf; it just means we must hunker down and get closer to the Lord.

Journal Time

The "I'm lonely" worship project:

Step 1, Begin to worship. Start by listening to worship music. Just listen to the words. Allow them to soak deep within yourself, and allow the music and melody minister to your spirit. As you allow the music to minister to your spirit, your spirit will begin to respond by wanting to worship the Lord in spirit and in truth.

Step 2, Thank God. Think about every positive thing you have in your life. Every time God said yes and every time He said no (this is ultimately a yes, but we will get to that later.) Begin to thank Him. It may start slow as you think of all the things you're thanking Him for, but as Holy Spirit drops things into your spirit about what has happened in your life, the thanks will flow freely.

As you praise, you will notice a renewing of your spirit. You will realize that God is there in the midst of all that you are going through. You will feel as though you are wrapped in the comfort and peace of the Holy Spirit.

Now get quiet and listen to what the Lord is trying to tell you.

Get out your journal and write it down.

Love Journey #2

Love, like you, won't be around tomorrow.
Love as THEIR life depended on it.
LOVE in spite of.
Love as Christ loved

Ignite love, live love, love fierce,

Tear down the walls that are keeping you from loving.

Kick fear in the teeth and love!

Stop being afraid, love. It's not painful,
It's one of the most beautiful things ever if you allow it to be.

The world has perverted one of the most extraordinarily beautiful things God created, true love.

Enduring love
Strong Love
Agape Love

EBONY N'TANTALA

Start your day right

Papa, show them the love You have for them. Let the person reading this book see themselves through Your eyes.

Affirm within yourself:

I WILL LOVE MYSELF; I WON'T LET ANYONE TELL ME I'M WORTHLESS, INCLUDING MYSELF! I CAN DO EXCEEDINGLY ABOVE WHAT THE WORLD HAS TOLD ME I CAN'T DO AS LONG AS I HAVE JESUS ON MY SIDE!!!

Ephesians 1:11

In him, we have obtained an inheritance, having been predestined according to the purpose of him who works all things According to the Counsel of his will

EBONY N'TANTALA

Chapter 3
Who are You?

According to Jeremiah 29:11, God says, "For I know the plans I have for you, declares the Lord, plans to prosper you and not harm you, plans to give you hope and a future."

Then in Psalms 139, he tells us we are fearfully and wonderfully made in His image.

2 Corinthians 5:17 tells us, "If anyone is in Christ, he

is a new creation, old things have passed away, behold all things have become new." You are new if you have accepted Christ as your Savior. You are no longer what the world has called you. You are loved, you are one of God's Chosen, and you're a Royal Priesthood. You are a joint heir with Christ. You are a Child of God. An ambassador for Christ. You are blessed. Get this in your spirit; know without a shadow of a doubt that you are precisely who God says you are. Stop allowing the foolish people in this world to tell you who you are and what you are. Once you accepted Christ, you became more than this world could handle. So, the world will try to convince you you're not up to par and tell you you're worthless. But you're not; you are the priceless love of God!

Love your uniqueness. Love how different God has made you. Improve yourself. Don't try to be anyone's mini-me. Be your very own you.

Journal Time

Truthfully answer the following questions.

1. Who do you think you are? Not So's, and So's mom or dad. Not the school nurse, not the CEO. But who are you?

2. Who do people think or say you are?

3. Who do you pretend to be?

4. Are you being the real you, or are you being "the you" you think everyone around you wants you to be?

5. Have you become so accustomed to living a false life that you don't know who you are?

Love Journey #3

Loving you means

You are aware of your flaws

And you love yourself anyway.
Loving you means,

You work on your flaws to make you better.
Loving you means,

you no longer listen to what people say about you,
You concentrate on what God has told you.

God has given you purpose; He calls you amazing and blessed.
Loving you means,
learning to see yourself as God sees you.

Beautifully blessed.

Isaiah 43:18-19

*"Remember not the
former things,
nor consider the things
of old.
19 Behold, I am doing
a new
thing; now it springs
forth,
do you not perceive it?
I will make a way in the
wilderness and rivers
in the desert.*

EBONY N'TANTALA

Chapter 4

Yesterday is Gone-
Beautifully Blessed

What can you do about yesterday?

Nothing, it is already gone. Well, that's not entirely true. If you have hurt people, you can ask for forgiveness. You can forgive yourself for your mistakes. You can learn from your mistakes and move on. Are there people you've hurt? Show them you've changed. Apologize (genuinely), ask for forgiveness, and keep it moving. Depending on where the person you have offended is in their life, they may or may not forgive you. But that doesn't mean you stay stuck in the past. You get up and move. Show the world you are a child of the Most High God. Don't allow things or people from your past to stop you from being who God has called you to be, including yourself.

So, you were a horrible person in your past. Have you changed? Have you learned from your mistakes? Have you moved on? Have you tried to show people who God is and how He changed your life for the better?

Or Maybe, you were the one they picked on in school. People made you feel like you weren't worth the time of day? Awesome, you're in great company. Christ was persecuted and criticized for being different, yet He didn't stay stuck in the hurt; He moved on. He accomplished what His Father called Him to do. We should strive for that, completing what God has placed us here to do.

    Learning to love you means you live for today and stop beating yourself up for your yesterdays. Move on, fix what you can, and keep moving. What's stopping you from moving forward? If it's your mindset, change it. If the problem is your friends, change them; if it's your family, set them aside for a minute. Nothing should stop you from accomplishing greatness, not even you! Get it together. There is Greater in you.

Journal Time

1. Did your past suck?
2. If yes, why?
3. Were you a horrible, promiscuous, mean, judgmental, or abusive person?
4. If yes, why?
5. Were you the one abused, picked on, or told you were less

than everyone else? If yes, when? How old were you? Do you still feel like that person? If you do still feel like that person, why?

Love Journey #4

Loving you means growing as you should and not allowing your past to define you.

If others choose to be complacent where they are, let them stay there by themselves; don't volunteer to join them there.
Don't continue to waste your energy on those who refuse to grow.
Love you enough to keep moving forward, even if it means leaving others behind.
Don't allow anyone to make

EBONY N'TANTALA

you feel guilty for moving forward and growing.

Psalm 139:13-14

For you formed my
inward parts; You knitted
me together in my
mother's
womb. I praise you, for
I am fearfully and
wonderfully made.
Wonderful
are your works;
my soul knows it
very well.

EBONY N'TANTALA

Chapter 5

You're an individual-Breaking the Mold

One of my favorite things about myself is I love being different! My thought processes are nothing like anyone here on Earth, and I love that I see things differently. I used to beat myself up because I was different and didn't see things the way people saw them.

My God, I was and still am the biggest nerd. And I

love every minute of it. I learned to stop cringing because of how different I was and began to embrace it. I embraced my individuality, uniqueness, and the undeniable rareness of me.

I wasn't happy when I tried to be like everyone else around me, and it stressed me out trying to keep up with what everyone was doing. The trends, the talk, the walk- it was way too much for me even to begin to see and know me for who I was.

One day, I looked at myself and realized I didn't like the "me" I was portraying. I hated everything about that person, the fake me, the "me" everyone wanted to see. So, I got rid of her. When she left, so did a lot of people who didn't like the real me. On my journey, I learned molds are best used for arts and crafts, and cookie cutters are best used on cookie dough, not people. God molded us in His image, the only mold we should adhere to. Not the mold the world is trying to get us to become. Over time I have learned that being who I am is a lot more freeing than trying to be like someone else.

    Loving you means being uniquely you! God designed you differently. You're outside and inside.
Don't try so hard to follow the crowd. Don't try to mimic or copy someone else, be you.

The unique, amazingly awesome you God designed you to be!

Journal Time

I. Who are you?
II. Who aren't you?
III. What are you striving for?
IV. What makes you unique?
V. Do you walk in your uniqueness?

Love Journey #5

Loving you; is breaking out of the mold the world

has for you! You're uniquely made and crafted to stand out. You are distinctive & beautiful! Allow yourself to stand out from everyone else. Love you enough to stand out and move forward.
The pack can't keep you bound; move around them. Move how God has called you to move.
Love you enough never to allow anyone to tell you you're not worth your individuality.
Love you enough to become what called you to be.

Love you enough to find your purpose of being placed in this world
Love you enough to fight for your love of yourself.
Love you enough to seek the value you possess on the inside.
You have seeds of purpose within you.
Love you enough to let them germinate and grow.

EBONY N'TANTALA

Psalm 139:7-10

Where shall I go from your Spirit? Or where shall I flee from your presence? If I ascend to heaven, you are there! If I make my bed in Sheol, you are there!

If I take the wings of the morning and dwell in the uttermost parts of the sea, even there, your hand shall lead me, and your right hand shall hold me.

Chapter 6

You are not alone

Have you ever felt no one hears you or No one ever realizes you're hurting? Do you feel you're going it alone? No one to turn to? And nowhere to go?

Look up, my friend; you're not alone, God – El Roi, the God who sees me, sees you. When you feel no one else sees you, no one else cares, God sees you, and He cares deeply about you and everything you do. He wants to hear about your day, about the people you want to fight and the people you want to love. He wants to hear about your future plans and how you plan to accomplish them. He wants you to cry to Him and allow Him to comfort you. You are not in this alone; you're not alone. God, who never sleeps and never slumbers, is always here to listen and comfort you.

Then you have Jesus, who is continually interceding on your behalf. At the same time, the Holy Spirit guides you and comforts you as you allow Him to. The hard part is for you to enable them to guide and lead you.

You must open your mouth, speak to Him, and let Him know your feelings. Then open your heart to hear what God is trying to say to you. Does He already know? Yes, he does. But in His infinite wisdom and love for you, God wants to hear straight from your mouth about what's going on in your life so that you know you are not alone. So you know He has not left you to wander or wonder alone.

God wants the best for your life, but if you don't, let Him in to help give you guidance and love. You will continuously feel like you are forever floundering in an ocean of loneliness and sorrow.

EBONY N'TANTALA

Journal Time

If you feel alone, even when people are around you, please explain why.

It's time for you to come clean. Write out what makes you feel lonely. What has kept you there all this time? Once you have written it down. Begin to pray about it and give it to God. Just hand it to Him.

And don't take it back.
Allow Papa to take the
loneliness away for good.
You can be alone or lonely
without feeling alone.

Love Journey #6

Loving you is knowing that the legacy you leave isn't for you but for those who come after you!

They are a part of you. Lay the foundation to allow them to stand. Truly loving you means making sure they are taken care of. Allowing your legacy of loneliness to be vanquished so that those who come after you know joy and peace even in lonely times

Psalm 127:1-2

Unless the LORD Builds the House A Song of Ascents. Of Solomon. Unless the LORD builds the house, those who build it labor in vain. Unless the LORD watches over the city, the watchman stays awake in vain. It is in vain that you rise up early and go late to rest, eating the bread of anxious toil; for he gives to his beloved sleep.

EBONY N'TANTALA

Chapter 7

It's okay to say No

(Set some boundaries)

Just because they ask you to help doesn't mean you have to. Are you like I used to be? Continually saying yes to everybody and everything just because you don't want to disappoint anyone. In the meantime, you're wearing yourself out because you're trying to be everything to everybody. This can be detrimental to your sanity, peace, and your life.

Just say NO! If you cannot do something because it will have you jumping through 10 hundred hoops, Say no and mean it. After saying No, don't allow the guilt of possibly hurting someone's feelings or disappointing someone to stop you from saying no and sticking to it. It's better to disappoint someone and keep a sound mind and health. Then hand over your peace of mind and health to make someone happy. This is called setting boundaries. Know what you can and cannot do, then stick to it. Remember, you must put your oxygen on first; sometimes, that means telling someone no and setting boundaries within yourself that will keep you safe.

EBONY N'TANTALA

Journal Time

1. How often do you say yes and wish you would've said no?
2. Why do you think it's hard to say no to others?
3. What are you going to do to let yourself know it's okay to say no?
4. What is the first boundary you are going to set for yourself?

Love Journey #7
Just say no!

Loving you means knowing when to say I can't do this anymore. Or I'm unable to do this! Knowing your limitations and speaking upon them keeps you from stressing over unnecessary things.

If you can't do something, say so. Do not overtax yourself. Do not let yourself become stressed out and overwhelmed because you took on much more than you could handle.

You saying no does not make

you less than others; it
makes you aware of yourself
and how much you can do
without stressing yourself
out.
Don't hurt yourself to please
someone else. Healthy
Boundaries are wonderful;
they protect you and the
other person. You will have
your space and time, and they
won't have to see you lose it
when you can't take it
anymore with the constant
demands of others around you.

Setting boundaries is a health hack. You will stress less and enjoy your life more.

EBONY N'TANTALA

1 Thessalonians 5:11

Therefore encourage

one another and

build one another up,

just as you are doing.

Chapter 8
Uplift someone who is in need

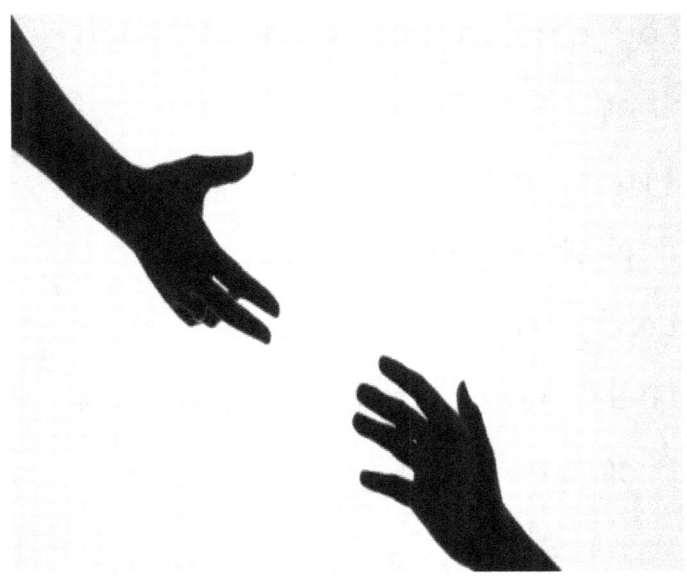

One thing I have found that helps me to feel better is making someone else's day! Help someone else feel better about themselves or their situation, showing them what God can do for them through them. Watching their eyes light up to see God's love for them and how much God truly loves and cares for them. How far they have come from where they started.

 *An important thing to remember here is to stay

within your boundaries. Do not go outside your "scope of peace" to help someone else find theirs.

This world tends to make us believe that we are to fight one another, not give love to one another, and not provide a hand up to someone who needs it because they may get ahead of us and do better than us. Humph, it is incredible that Jesus wanted us to do greater things than Him. John 14:12 (ESV) says: "Truly, truly I say to you whoever believes in me will also do the works that I do; and GREATER works than these will he do because I am going to the Father."

So, if Christ is willing to uplift us so we can do greater works than He did, why wouldn't we want the same for those we help?

Journal Time

1. Are you so wrapped up in yourself that you can't see when someone else is hurting or needs love?
2. Does fear have you trapped into believing if you help someone, they will always need you? Or they may become more significant than you?

3. Have you forgone helping someone because you fear them becoming more significant than you?

Love Journey #8

Men and women can love and uplift one another without gossip, competition, or pettiness.

When you find someone, you can enjoy the love of Christ with, without any foolery; it's amazingly beautiful.

The love of God is NOT forceful; it's not mean, it's not making some feel less than others, and it's not placing fear in the hearts of

those who surround you.
It's uplifting, peaceful, joyful, edifying, and may convict your heart, but it will never condemn it.

Ephesians 2:10(ESV)

For we are his workmanship, created in Christ Jesus for good works, which God prepared beforehand, that we should walk in them.

EBONY N'TANTALA

Chapter 9

POETRY IN MOTION

Did you know; before you were born, your life was written in the stars? Papa, God created the beautiful poem of you, so all could see how amazingly beautiful you are.

Workmanship in Greek is poiēma or in the English poem.

Ephesians 2:10 says for we are his workmanship, created in Christ Jesus unto good works, which God hath before ordained that we should walk in them.

So we are literally poems; God is writing. HOW AWESOME IS THAT!

We have verses and stanzas. Conjunctions, adjectives, nouns, verbs, pronouns.

Lyrically God is narrating our stories.

With His hands, He is directing our paths.

I DON'T KNOW ABOUT Y'ALL, BUT I'M SO GLAD I AM SAVED.

Journal Time

1. Think about a time when God showed you how amazing you are.
2. What was it?
3. Were you able to think about anything?

If not, that's because you've never looked at yourself through God's eyes. Papa, if they haven't seen themselves through Your eyes. Open

their eyes so they can
see what You see in them.

Love Journey #9

Realizing I am fearfully and wonderfully made by the hands of God.
He gave me a purpose; no one can take away. He shows me genuine love, daily.
His correction lengthens my years and lifts my soul.
His peace hugs me tight when hell is breaking loose around me.
His joy covers me in my saddest times.

The love God has for me can never be taken away.

He values my life and shows me how to value my life, as well.

He shows me I'm precious in His sight and loved by Him for eternity.

He loves exceptionally different from the world!

I was made to be loved, and so were you.

EBONY N'TANTALA

Hebrews 12:6-10

For the Lord disciplines,
the one he loves and
chastises every son whom
he receives"
It is for discipline that
you Have to endure. God
is treating you as sons.
For what son is
there whom his Father does
not discipline?
If you are left without
discipline, in which
all have participated,
then you are
illegitimate children

and not sons. Besides
this, we have had earthly
fathers who disciplined us,
and we respected them.
Shall we not much more
be subject to the
Father of spirits and
live? For they
disciplined us for a
short time as it seemed
best to them, but he
disciplines us for
our good, that we may share

His holiness.

EBONY N'TANTALA

Chapter 10

We All Need Correction

Correction is a noun meaning a change that rectifies an error or inaccuracy (Oxford Dictionary online)

I know you're grown, and no one can tell you what to do. At least, that's what many adults believe—unknowingly passing that same thought pattern to their children. The: "You can't tell me what to do" mentally.

Have you noticed you are stuck? Not moving far in life? It's because you need direction. With direction comes correction.

We do things that can cause us harm, could cause others harm, or are not within the will of The Lord. He takes the time to let us know we are wrong. It may come in the form of someone physically coming to you and letting you know your actions are wrong. Other times, you have to find out on your own what you are doing is wrong. This process can be quick or take several years. The method of being corrected can be painful, but it heals and develops us in a way that only the will of God can.

The Bible states God does not correct those He doesn't love. So be grateful when God sends correction your way. He is showing you; you are loved by the author of love.

Journal Time

1. Think of the times your earthly parents have corrected you. Did they help you to become a better person?
2. Think of a time; the Lord corrected you. How has that correction shaped your life?

Love Journey #10

Correction, correction, correction

Loving you means realizing on your love journey, accepting correction is the beginning of finding your purpose and value.

not every cause is your cause

Not every problem is yours to fix.

EBONY N'TANTALA

Matthew 6:33

But seek first the

kingdom of God and

his

righteousness, and all

these things will

be added to you.

Chapter 11

Consult the Chief Consultant

EBONY N'TANTALA

We all do it, call our mom, dad, sister, brother, or best friend to get advice that may not be from the Lord, to satisfy our inner self that told us we need to ask about it.

We're asking everybody and their grandma, but we forget to consult the One who wants our lives to be the best they can be for us while we are here on Earth. No, He never said life would be easy, but He did say that if we seek His Kingdom first before we buy that car, that house, or date that man or woman, we could have a better outcome than us running off all willy-nilly to everyone else but Him.

When we seek the advice or direction of the Lord, our outcomes are more favorable, without the pitfalls that come from seeking everywhere but His Kingdom. The best advice we can get is from the One who is continually writing the poem of us.

Journal Time

1. When was a time you wished you would have consulted God about a situation in your life?
2. How has your life been different because of not consulting God?

Remember, all journal entries allow you to see your shortcomings and strengths.

Love Journey #11
Loving you means learning;

not all things are for you, even if you can do it. Sometimes you have to slow down, pause, and see what happens next before you jump the gun on what your head says you want to do.
Ask God; if He says yes, roll with it, baby. But not before.
Loving you means learning self-control even when you just got to have it, or you can't live without it. Timing is everything, and everything has a perfect time.

EBONY N'TANTALA

You will have your heart's desire when your heart is truly ready to receive.

Isaiah 53:5

But he was pierced for our transgressions;

he was crushed for

our iniquities;

upon him was the

chastisement that

brought us peace and with his wounds,

we are healed.

Chapter 12

Healing and Deliverance

Healing is a great way to keep yourself going on your love journey. So many things within you have made you the way you are. It's time to let them go. Get set free from the shame, guilt, pain, and hurt! Let that mess go!! I'm talking about getting that deep-down true deliverance that makes demons cower in response because they know you are about to grow into exactly who God has called you to be. Woooo! Let's Go!! If you can't do this on your own, ask for help. Only ask for help from a man or woman of God who truly knows the Lord and can hear what says the Lord. Several therapists in your area or even online are Kingdom of God-loving folks who can help you eliminate the mess you are holding onto.

What has happened in your life that has made you so fearful? What or who has made you forget your first love? What life-changing event have you stuck in the depression and anxiety you suffer? You don't know? Seek help.

Let me debunk something for all of the overly spiritual Christians out there. There is nothing wrong with Jesus and the therapist. If you can have Jesus and a doctor to help heal your body, then having Jesus and a therapist to help heal your mind is fine too. If your doctor can prescribe medication to help heal your body, then a therapist can prescribe medication to help regulate and heal your mind.

If you're afraid to talk to people for help, begin by getting help from the Lord. Ask Him where you became worried. What events brought you to the point of why you no longer trust? And even which therapist to see. It's time to let things go so you can fill yourself with the peace, love, and joy only the Lord can bring. Allow God to deliver you from all that torments you.

Remember, you are worth it to be truly free. Your life and everyone in it, especially you, will be grateful for it.

Journal Time

1. What's holding you back?

2. Do you want to be delivered from it?

3. Are you ready for it to go?

4. What would your life be like without…?

EBONY N'TANTALA

Love Journey #12

Loving yourself is knowing deliverance is the beginning of your freedom journey. Now that you've been delivered seek inner healing.

To truly move forward in freedom, love, and peace, you must be healed from what caused you so much pain for many years.

Mark 12:31

*The second is this: '
You shall love*

your neighbor as yourself.

There is no other

*commandment
greater than these."*

Chapter 13

ME, DAY!!!!

Yep, you read that right. Today is all about you. If not today, then a day real soon. We must realize that continually caring for everyone else and not ourselves makes us stressed, exhausted, and downright mean.

Allow people to see that even in your busy life of ministry, work, school, kids, and running a business, you take time for yourself. Baby, it's okay!

Assisting people before you help yourself is like; being stuck with someone in quicksand. You make sure they get out safely while you slowly sink to the bottom because; both of you are too tired to help you get out.

If you are so busy concentrating on helping someone else get better but never look at yourself to get better first, are you being beneficial to them?

Trust me, even though your family may pout and act

like the world is falling apart because you've decided to take time for yourself, it won't. Enjoy some time for yourself. In the end, you and your family will be grateful for it.

Journal Time

What are you going to do on your ME DAYS?

Make a list of all the things you would like to do on your days that it's all about you.

Remember, it doesn't have to be an entire day. It can be as little as 30 mins as long as it is time you have set aside for yourself

Love Journey #13

Take time for yourself!

Loving you means knowing you're allowed to take a break. Give yourself an hour. Twice a week, and love on you!

Sit with a cup of coffee and converse with The Lord.

Write down your accomplishments.

Write about what you want to accomplish.

Dance till your heart's content

Take a walk.

Take a nap

EBONY N'TANTALA

Get a massage

Get your nails done.

Read a book

Do something for yourself.

Work up to 1 hour once a week.

James 5:16-20 (ESV)

Therefore, confess your sins to one another and pray for one another that you may be healed.

The prayer of a righteous person has great power as it is working.

Elijah was a man with a nature like ours, and he prayed fervently that it might not rain, and for three years and six months, it did not rain on the Earth. Then he prayed again, and heaven gave rain and the earth bore its fruit.

My brothers, if anyone among you wanders from the truth, and someone brings him back, let him know that whoever brings back a

EBONY N'TANTALA

sinner from his wandering will save his soul from death multitude of sins.

Chapter 14

Who's Your Crew?

The people you are around should be those who lift you and tell you the truth in love. This means correcting you when you're wrong and showing you who you are in the eyes of God. They should not use correction to degrade or condemn. You should like just being around them because of who they are, and they should enjoy being around you just because of who you are.

If the people you hang out with make you feel

stagnate or worse than you felt before you were around them, then maybe it's time you change the people in your crew.

Remember boundaries and peace of mind are paramount in learning to love who you are. If the people you hang out with don't know how to respect the boundaries you place, you do NOT need to be around them. If the people you hang out with can't seem to do anything but pull you into their messy life with them. Then it is time to change who your crew is.

You realize that God has boundaries, and for us to enjoy time in his presence, we must comply with those boundaries. If we want to be a part of God's crew, we must accept Christ as our Savior. We must believe that Christ is the Son of God and that He rose on the 3rd day so that one day we could go hang out with God in Heaven and be our intercessor while we are living here on Earth. We must not have sin on us. We can be a part of God's crew because He looks at us through Christ. And being a part of His crew, He will correct us in love and uplift us, showing us how we look through His eyes.

If you are having difficulty figuring out who should or should not be in your crew, hang out with God for a bit; you will be amazed at what He will show and tell you.

Journal Time

1. Who's your crew?
2. Who are the ones you can be yourself around?
3. Do you have anyone you can be yourself with no pretenses?
4. If not, what do you need to get out of the way to get there?

Love Journey #14

Loving you means hanging out with those you love and truly just enjoying your time spent with them. Life on Earth goes quickly; enjoy every aspect of it.

`Hang out with God for a bit; you will be amazed at what He will tell you.

Ephesians 3:16-19

I ask that out of the riches of His glory, He may strengthen you with power through His Spirit in your inner being, so that Christ may dwell in your hearts through faith. Then you, being rooted and grounded in love, will have power, together, with all the saints, to comprehend the length and width and height and depth... of the love of Christ, and to know this love that surpasses knowledge, that you may be filled with all the fullness of God.

Chapter 15
The Measure of it All

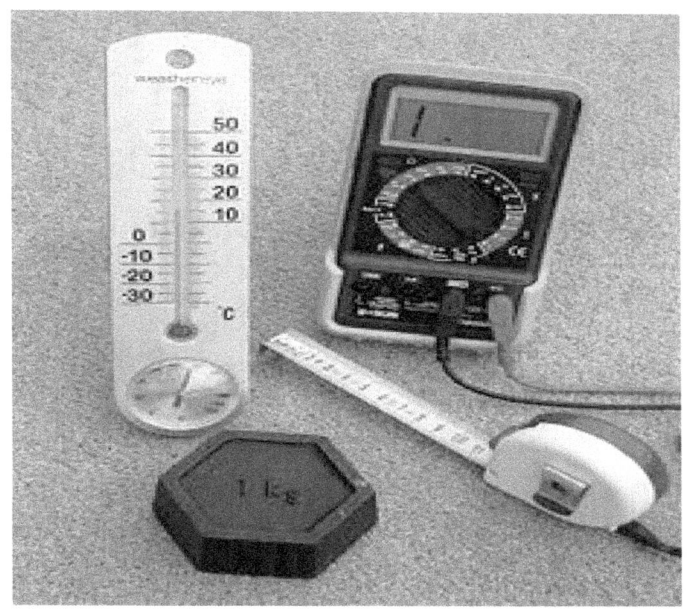

Love has no depth, height, or width. Do not profess love if you plan on measuring it by the world's standards. The world says love them as much as they love you. The world says, love them till you get tired of them. Love them until they change from who they were when you first met them. Love them for what they can do for you. This is what the world says love is.

God says love is brand new mercies and grace each

and every morning. God says love is His son dying on the cross so that you can live a life with Him for all eternity. God says love is, even in your sin, He loved you. God says love is never leaving or forsaking you.

God allows Love to be placed in front of you daily, called mercy and grace. Embrace it roll in it, rejoice in it, be grateful for it, and praise God for it!

Love outside the storm, love inside the storm, and in

the eye of the storm. If you find yourself only wanting to do for others because of what they can do for you. You need to check your love meter. What are you measuring your love with? Is it the acts they can do for you? Or the Heart of God within you?

Journal Time

1. Do you measure the love that someone gives you or the love you give to someone else?

2. Are you doing a tit-for-tat with your loved one?

3. What has made you this way?

4. Why do you feel more protected this way?

Remember your journal entries are for you to be truthful with yourself and to help you grow throughout your love journey,

Love Journey #15

Check your heart motives.
Loving you means being honest with yourself. If your motives or heart posture are wrong, you need to check yourself.

Look on the inside and check your own heart.
Are you genuinely loving, caring, giving, and supportive because that's what you want to do? Or are you doing it to reap the benefits of it?

If you don't want to be hurt by someone's lack of character, you must check your character and motives. Don't act one way in front of those you deem essential and another way to those you feel are unworthy.
In other words, don't be fake.

EBONY N'TANTALA

Psalms 37:4-5

Delight yourself in the

Lord and He will

Give you the

desires of your heart.

Commit your way to the

Lord; trust in Him

and He will act.

Chapter 16

Knowing your heart's desire

Psalms 37:4 tells us if we delight ourselves in the Lord, you know, spend that quality time with Him and hang out with Him and Love Him just cause He's God; He will give us the desires of our heart. God's Word won't return void. So hang out with Him and see.

My grandchildren are two of my heartbeats. I love how they love me just because I'm Yaya. Just hanging out and loving on me because it's where they feel safe and comfortable. It's where they can get love from.

It's the same way with God. He loves hanging out with us and loves when we love Him just because He's God. He loves when we come to Him for comfort and love. He loves when we talk to Him telling Him our secrets and our dreams.

When you spend quality time with God, He will begin to show you your true heart's desires, encourage you to ask for them, and show you how to work towards them if they are within His will. If they are not within His will, He will show how it isn't in His will and convict your heart all at the same time while He is loving and correcting you.

Write down your true heart's desires, not the fly-by-night ones but your real heart's desire, the things you burn for. Believe God will direct you in them. If they are of His will, He will grant them. If they are not of His will, He will convict your heart and explain why you aren't in His will.

If you don't know your heart's desire, ask God. Or begin to write the things you like. The more you write, the more you discern the "fly by night" desires from your true deep-down desires.

Journal Time

What are your heart's true desires?

Dig deep! Find the things you've longed for but have pushed to the back burner of your life. Be real transparent with yourself.

Love Journey #16

Loving you means knowing the desires of your heart, writing them down, praying over them and believing in them, and having the faith to know God will give you the desires of your heart.

EBONY N'TANTALA

Mark 4:22

For nothing is hidden

except to be made manifest,

nor is anything

secret except to come to

light.

Chapter 17

Don't Keep Secrets

A secret here, a secret there, little secrets, big secrets, a sprinkle of secrets everywhere. The enemy uses them to keep you bogged down and afraid. They can make you bitter, they can make you fearful, and they can make you stay stuck in the place where the secret was born.

I'm not saying run and tell everyone under the sun your business. But, you should confide in someone you trust to tell your secrets to. If you fear something being found out, you must reveal it yourself before someone else reveals it, making things worse than they are. When someone else tells your secrets, it makes you vulnerable involuntarily, making you lash out and not think clearly about what is happening around you or who may be watching how you handle your involuntary vulnerability.

When you tell your secret your way, you are voluntarily

vulnerable, freeing yourself from the shackles of hurt, fear, and shame. Those people who are watching you will become inspired by the freedom you've gained from your voluntary vulnerability.

None of us are perfect, so telling people who you used to be is okay. It's okay for people to see how far you have come in your walk. It's okay for people to see your growth. It's okay if you have a past. If you run into people who don't think it's okay, that's fine too. Not everyone is for you. Everyone isn't going to be your friend. Trust me; you don't want the ones who can't see past who you used to be. Those are usually people who are hiding from their own secret past.

When you are ready to reveal yourself to others, pray about it first. Ask the Lord who you should talk to and when you should speak to them. There is always a time, place, and season for you to open up about your past secrets. Listen to God and allow God to give you the steps to go forward with being set free from your secrets. When you're set free from those, there is nothing the enemy can hold over your head.

Journal Time

1. What have you kept hidden deep down that you're afraid or ashamed of exposing?
2. Have you taken this to the Lord?
3. Have you become a different person since this incident?
4. Can this incident and your outcome improve someone else's life if you ministered to them using your situation?

God can use everything that happens in our lives to help someone else.

Journal truthfully. It will help free you. Pray over it, give it all to God, and leave it there; wait for Him to tell you what your next steps should be.

Love Journey #17

Love yourself enough to stop allowing things to plague you.

A plague will smite, infest, or afflict you with a disease, calamity, or natural evil. To cause one to worry or distress.

When you see a plague, get rid of it ASAP before it destroys you.

Be like Phineas; once you see the source of the plague, stop it in its tracks!!!

Habakkuk 2:2-3 (ESV)

And the Lord answered me:

"Write the vision;

Make it plain on tablets,

so he may run who reads it.

For still the vision awaits

its appointed time;

it hastens to the end—it

will not lie. If it seems slow,

wait for it; it will

surely come; it will not delay.

Chapter 18

Write your Vision

Have you ever noticed that some of the most successful businesses have a plan and vision for the company? A business plan helps a company to move towards something. If you don't have a vision, you tend to work in circles, not knowing where you're going or your goal.

In Proverbs 29:18a (ESV), Solomon says, "Where there is no vision, the people cast off restraint." In the Hebrew study bible, it says, "In the absence of a vision, the people will be dismayed." In other words, without a vision, we tend to stress ourselves out. If you followed a plan, and no, it doesn't have to be to the letter; it can change over time. But if you have a blueprint of what you want to do and where you want to be, you will not sweat the small things that don't matter. It helps to get rid of unnecessary busywork. It keeps you focused on your goal even when you get off track.

Journal Time

Okay, y'all, this is big! It's time to write your vision. Keep it simple for now; configure or elaborate on it as you see fit. The point is to have something to go by to help keep you focused.

Love Journey #18

Love yourself enough to write down and commit it to memory your vision. Your vision is important to God; after all, He gave it to you. Don't allow yourself to get so caught up in someone else's dream you forget about your own

EBONY N'TANTALA

Psalms 27:1

The Lord is my light and my salvation Whom shall I fear? The Lord is the stronghold of my life; of whom shall I be afraid?

2 Timothy 1:7

For the spirit God gave us does not make us timid, but gives us power, love and self-discipline

Chapter 19
Punch Fear in the Face

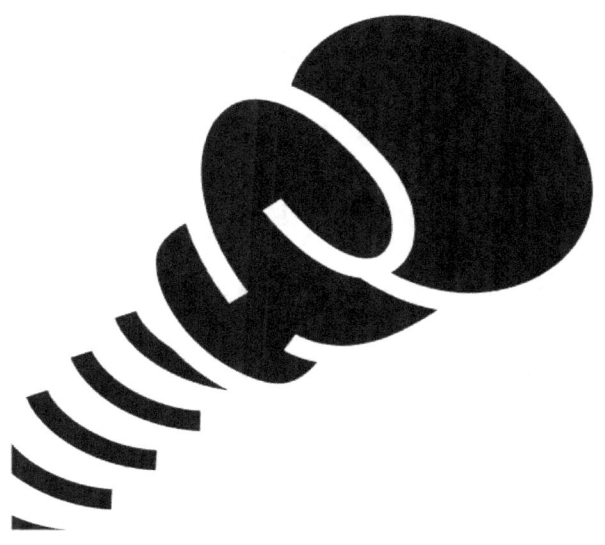

Lace 'em up, lace 'em up! Look fear in the face and tell it; it no longer has a hold on you. Hallelujah! Nothing can stop you unless you allow it to stop you. Fear truly is <u>f</u>alse <u>e</u>vidence <u>a</u>ppearing <u>r</u>eal! God has given us authority over the Earth, and there should be nothing that we should fear. Hey Glory!

Fighting fear has become one of the things I love to teach. People do not realize that fear is responsible for many things that keep people bound. Fear has little friends that hang out with him; some of their names are racism, depression, anxiety, and pride, to name a few. Do you realize that poverty is also in with fear? Some people fear becoming all that God has called them to be because they will lose assistance, or they have a fear of failure as they try to keep up with what God has called them to do. Or they fear losing the people they have been around for years.

Psalms 34:4 says, "I sought the Lord, He answered me and delivered me from all my fears" The first thing we see is the writer states he sought the Lord, and He (the Lord) delivered him from all his fears. He sought the Lord. Have you sought the Lord? Seek ye first the kingdom of God. Seek God. He gave us the authority to trample on serpents. Are you allowing fear to be a serpent that wraps itself around you, slowly suffocating you waiting to strike with its death blow? Step on its head! You do NOT have to live that way! You do NOT have to allow it to stay.

    The only fear we should have is the fear of the Lord. What are you fearing? Why are you allowing it to stop you? For the Lord is your strength if YOU allow Him to be. We become fearful because we try to take on things on our own when we should turn them over to

The Lord. Give that stuff to the stronger One and leave it there.

Know this, staying in poverty is not of God, and He does not want you there. And I'm not just talking about monetary poverty; I'm also talking about mental, emotional, and spiritual poverty. Learn and grow as God has called you to do. When fear has nowhere to work, he will flee from you. Pray that you can and will do all things through Christ who strengthens you. It's time to teach this annoying spirit who truly is the boss around here. Amen!!!

Journal Time

Call out and write down all those things you fear, from the smallest to the greatest. Don't allow any of it to stay. Tell all of it; it has to go. Give it to the Lord and allow Him to dispose of it. Don't you dare pick it back up!

Let's GO! Punch Fear in the FACE!!!

Love Journey # 19

Loving yourself means punching fear in the face and living your dream! The more impossible, the better. God got this; you just stand in faith, believing He can, and He will do exceedingly, abundantly above what you could ask or think!

Matthew 5:14-16

"You are the light of the world. A city set on a hill cannot be hidden. Nor do people light a lamp and put it under a basket, but on a stand, and it gives light to all in the house. In the same way, let your light shine before others so that they may see your good works and give glory to your Father, who is in heaven.

EBONY N'TANTALA

Chapter 20

Come Out of the Cave

Day twenty, you've arrived. You're getting closer to learning who you are and what you are called to do.

Olly Olly oxen free, you can come out now. You can stop hiding from who you are. Why are you hiding from yourself? What you're hiding from? Have you figured out what's keeping you in that cave? Are you making a true effort to change your life? Come out of the cave. Don't let THINGS keep you bound!

Don't allow the lies spoken over your life to keep you hidden and in bondage all your life! Come out and see what God is doing for you! Come out of the cave and see where God wants to take you. Come out of the cave and see what the future holds.

You won't be able to see any of it unless you decide to come out of the cave into Christ's glorious light.

Journal Time

1. What are you holding onto?
2. Why are you holding on to it?
3. What lie do you believe about yourself?
4. Are you ready to come out of the cave?

Love Journey #20

Loving yourself means eliminating the lies and leaving the cave you've been trapped in for so long. God didn't call you to stay hidden; he called you to shine, to be His messenger, his mouthpiece. Don't let the lies, guilt, and shame of your past keep you in bondage in your future.

Philippians 3:13-14

Brothers, I do not
consider that I have
made it my own.
But one thing I do:
forgetting what lies
behind and straining
forward to
what lies ahead

EBONY N'TANTALA

Chapter 21

Let it All go

Loving yourself means
letting go of the things that

are destroying you from the inside out. Holding onto bitterness, anger, unforgiveness, envy, strife, and grudges doesn't help you. It hinders you and stunts your growth. It causes you to deteriorate from the inside out, slowly destroying your mind and body.

What is it giving us except heartache, anger, continual pain, bitterness, and in some cases, rage? Why hold on to something whose job is to destroy you? All of these things stress you out; stress is the silent killer. No one sees it as a culprit, but it silently kills you, sometimes slowly, in other cases fast.

Stop allowing THINGS to stunt your growth! Stop this slow and emotional, physical, and spiritual suicide.

Journal Time

1. What are you allowing to stunt your growth?
2. What is keeping you from reaching your full potential in the Lord?

Love Journey #21

I'm so glad the Tales of my anger, mistrust, bitterness, rage, loneliness, heartache, and pain are being worked on by me in the natural, while God cleanses me with the Blood of Christ in the Spiritual. It's learning even when I gave up on me, God carried me through the storms; He believed I could when I knew I couldn't!

Have to love the journey that makes you stronger!!!!

Galatians 1:10 (ESV)

For am I now seeking the approval of man, or of God? Or am I trying to please man? If I were still trying to please man, I would not be a servant of Christ.

Chapter 22

STOP IT ALREADY

Life is too short to try and please people continually. The sad part is that most people you are trying to please don't even like you!! Please, God Only!!!

People will speak ill of you at some point and time. So what!? Get over it. Some people have no life and must be mean and wag their tongues about someone to survive. (Yep, I said that). If people mean you well, they will correct you in love, not condemnation.

God should be the only One we worry about pleasing. Not one of these folks down here can get you into heaven.

So when they talk about you, cry a little if you must. But then brush it off or use it as a stepping stone to get to where God has called you to be. It's time to see higher.

Journal Time

1. Do you find yourself trying to please people?
2. Are these people you are trying to please significant in your life?
3. If so, why do you feel the need to please them?
4. How does trying to please this person or people make you feel?

5. Do you try to please God as much as you do people?

Remember to be truthful in your journal; it is for you to go back a look over to see how far you've come on your journey.

Love Journey #22

Loving you means no longer trying to please the crowd. Do what God has called you to. Who cares what others think? They won't be the ones answering to God on judgment day as to why you didn't complete what He called you to do. That's all on you, boo! So thank them and do what God said. He will deal with them later.

Proverbs 18:20-21

From the fruit of
a man's mouth his
stomach is satisfied;
he is satisfied by
the yield of his lips.
Death and life are
in the power of the
tongue, and those
who love it will
eat its fruits.

Chapter 23

Speak life

In January 2020, my son was DOA when he arrived at the hospital. His friend called me and told me, "TJ's dead. They don't know if he will live; they're in there working on him now."

All I could say was, "No, he's not. He will be fine; what is his blood pressure?" I couldn't bring myself to say my son was dead, and I refused to believe it. I refused to claim it. I told his nurse I spoke to, "Go tell my son he will live and not die." I told his nurse to "speak life over him and don't stop speaking life over him."

I'm happy to say that God said "yes." My son is alive and well. He had no traumatic brain injuries, as they told me he would have. He is still planning on finishing vet school and believes he will continue all that he started and more. I continue to pray over him that he lives the life God has called him to live.

Speak life in every situation; every problem speaks life. Speak life over your finances and home. Speak life over your job or your company.

Speak life over those you love and those you can't stand.

Use your tongue as a weapon to speak life into your life and those around you.

Your tongue can be a weapon of mass destruction or an instrument of healing. Wisely choose how you use it because you will have to eat the fruit of what you have spoken.

Journal Time

Take this time to begin to speak life over yourself and your family. Speak life to all those things God has told you; you would accomplish. If you haven't been speaking life over the things you hold dear, let this be the beginning of your life-speaking journey as you find love for yourself in your love journey.

Listen to worship or soaking music to set the atmosphere. Write down what or who you spoke life over.

Love Journey #23

Loving you means speaking life and not death over you and all you love and care for. Speak life over this nation, over your job. In everything, SPEAK LIFE.

Revelation 3:20-22 (ESV)

Behold, I stand at the door and knock.

If anyone hears my voice and opens the door,
I will come into him

and eat with him, and he with me.

The one who conquers, I will grant him to sit with me on my throne, as I also conquered and sat down with my Father on his throne.
He who has an ear, let him
hear what the Spirit says to the churches.

Chapter 24

Open your Heart

It's time to open your heart and see God wants what's best for you. No more excuses or more B.S. reasons why you believe God doesn't love you. NO more foolish talk of why you can't go on or move on in your walk. Do you know the Holy Spirit can give you direction in your walk? All you have to do is ask. We are all guilty of believing we can go it alone. But God sent the Holy Spirit to be our comforter and direction giver.

Remember, the Lord will never leave or forsake you, even when you have left and forgotten about Him. If you draw near to God, He will draw near to you.

When you forget who God is, He still remembers you. You've just become too blind to realize or recognize it.

Journal Time

1. what is God showing you that you have forgotten?

2. what promises have you closed your eyes and your heart to because they didn't come in your timing?

Love Journey #24

Loving you means

Open your eyes and see the love God has for you.

Open your heart and know. He is waiting to set you free.

EBONY N'TANTALA

2 Corinthians 12:9

But he said to me,
"My grace is
sufficient for you,
for my power
is made perfect
in weakness."
Therefore I will
boast all the
more gladly of
my weaknesses,
so that the power of
Christ may
rest upon me.

Chapter 25

Moving Forward

Don't look back now! You should only look back to remember where you came from and how much you've grown! Don't you dare stop!! Yes, it's hard. Yes, it's tiring! Yes, it seems impossible. But that's where Christ shows his strength. He says in His word where we are weak, He is strong.

Allow Christ to be the strength you use to keep moving forward. Don't stop, don't stop, don't stop! Keep going; keep moving. Love on you, and believe in what God has placed within you. Greater is He who is within you than He that is in the world. Eyes Forward, no looking back, let's prepare and see for what may be coming next.

Journal Time

1. If you can't believe in yourself, believe in the Christ who saved your soul.
2. Believe in the God who sent His Son to die in your place.
3. Write 20 things that are great about you.
4. Write five things you want to accomplish within the next six months.

Love Journey #25

Loving yourself means remembering where you came from and what you've come through and not allowing it to keep you bound in that place.

Move forward; don't allow death to take you before your time.

Ephesians 1:4-5

Even as He chose us
in Him before the
foundation of the
world that we should be
holy and blameless before Him. In
love,
he predestined us
for adoption to Himself as sons
through
Jesus Christ, according
to the purpose of His will.

Chapter 26

Christ isn't going anywhere

Have you been striving to get it right? Making several mistakes along the way, then beating yourself up because of them? So you haven't gotten it right yet. So what. Have you stopped trying? Unless you're perfect, it may take several times to get something right. A Fail is only a failure when you quit and don't try. Begin to view failure as a stepping stone to getting it right.

You have a choice in life; you can learn to build things up or tear them down. The wild thing about what I just said is you can take either part as positive or negative. You can build things up and help them grow. Or you can build things up to keep yourself isolated. But since we are learning to love ourselves to love others, there will be no isolation. In the second part, you can tear down the things holding you hostage and keeping you in bondage, or you can tear down things that have made you grow because you're afraid of what you can't see. But, since we are learning to love ourselves, flaws and all, there will be no tearing down due to fear. Amen!

Remember, Romans 8:28 says, "All things work together for good for those who are called according to His purpose." Your failures are stepping stones to a better future. Look at every successful company, Tesla didn't get it right the first several times, but he never stopped. He built from the failures and used them as stepping stones to make Tesla what it is today.

So, it's your choice; you can use your failures as tombstones to bury you or stepping stones to get you to your goal.

Journal Time

1. What are you tearing down? Is it positive or negative?
2. What are you building up? Is it positive or negative?

Remember, all journal entries are for your growth. They are not for you to impress anyone but for you to learn about yourself and for you to see how far you've come on your love journey.

Love Journey #26

Loving yourself means not counting yourself or God out of the equation.

You didn't get it right today; try again tomorrow. And the next day, just don't give up on you.

God may be moving slower than you like, but He moves as fast as you need Him to in this season.

He has heard you. Get in position, believe God will, and be prepared for Him to blow your mind!

Proverbs 3:5-7

Trust in the LORD with all your heart, and do not lean on your own understanding. In all your ways acknowledge him, and he will make straight your paths. Be not wise in your own eyes; fear the LORD, and turn away from evil.

Chapter 27

You're Powerful, Stand Out

Learn to use the wisdom God has given you. What, you feel as though you don't have any wisdom? Have you asked God for it? Your love for the Lord is the first step in finding wisdom.

It's time to exercise that wisdom and lean on the Lord for all your needs. The Bible says we should seek first the kingdom of God and all its righteousness, and all things will be added unto us. You learned you're an individual earlier in the journey, and now, you need to find your power within your individualism.

Don't follow the crowd, be your own voice, and speak up when God tells you to. Jesus told the disciples in Matthew 10, do not be anxious, how you are to speak or what you are to say, for what you are to say will be given to you in that hour. For it's not you who speak, but the Spirit of your Father speaking through you. Your strength comes from within.

Love your strength as well as your weaknesses; they are what make you the unique individual you were called to be.

Journal Time

Take time to write down what makes you the unique individual God has made you. No one or two lines, but go deep and find the amazing and unique individual you are.

Love Journey #27

Loving you means not following the crowd. Don't make anyone or anything on this Earth your idol. That includes political parties and candidates. Those folks are just like you. Don't worship anything created by the Creator. It's like slapping God in the face saying He isn't good enough for you.

Stand out, speak out. Love folks for the Love of God, not the love of people.

EBONY N'TANTALA

Mark 16:14-15

Afterward, he appeared to the eleven themselves as they were reclining at table, and he rebuked them for their unbelief and hardness of heart, because they had not believed those who saw him after he had risen. And, he said to them, "Go into all the world and proclaim the gospel to the whole creation.

Chapter 28

Don't Just Sit There

Learn to stop sitting back and waiting for your time to go to heaven while watching others who don't know the Lord suffer. Stop solely relying on the word of man instead of the Word of the Lord. Refuse to be satisfied with the mediocrity of home, work, church, and home again, only to repeat the cycle.

Refuse to allow others to dictate what we can and cannot do. Refuse to allow fear to control your movements. Refuse to make anything created by the Creator, an idol.

Learn to listen and move as GOD gives you direction. Place your faith and trust in The Holy Spirit. Now that you are learning to love yourself, you can begin to love as God tells you to love. Learn to forgive those who have wrongfully accused you. Know in your heart; you will go further than you ever thought.

EBONY N'TANTALA

By faith, believe, and by faith, love, and live. Don't allow yourself to be the ones who are SAVED, SATISFIED, AND SITTING!!

Journal Time

Come on now, tell the truth. Are you satisfied knowing you're saved and having your "pass" to go to heaven?

If not, what can you do to do better?

If yes, why? Are you willing to change? If not, why?

Love Journey #28

Me loving me means I refuse to be Saved, Satisfied, and Sitting! God has given me promises, and I plan on seeing them come to fruition.

Proverbs 13:3

Whoever guards his mouth preserves his life; he who opens wide his lips comes to ruin.

Matthew 12:36-37

I tell you, on the day of judgment people will give account for every careless word they speak, for by your words you will be justified, and by your words you will be condemned.

EBONY N'TANTALA

Chapter 29

Take out the Trash

Trash talkers, name-callers, they don't belong in your atmosphere. They intimidate and bring the spirit of fear and low self-esteem with them—the constant fear of being less than others stands out vividly in their minds. So to cover it up, they use fear and low self-esteem to beat up others verbally. Get away from these people. If you can't, ignore them as much as possible. But always remember to pray for them. They have more going on inside of them that they are too afraid to reveal. Forgive them so you can be set free.

Once God opened my eyes and showed me the smiles on many faces were fake, the tears rolled down my cheeks; my heart broke a bit because I believe that everyone has some good in them; humph, non are good who don't have Christ. Yet, I want to see the smiles on their faces, I want them to know Jesus is real and He can make the most hateful person happy, but the human condition blinds many, and only a few will ever see what it means to be truly free.

Journal Time

1. Have you forgiven your bully? I don't care who it is or was; have you forgiven them?

2. Are you still holding a grudge against them?

3. Remember, we spoke earlier about letting go of things. Is this one of the things you need to let go of?

OR

1. Are you the bully?

2. What are you holding or to?

3. What are you afraid of people seeing? Remember, this journal is for letting go and learning to love yourself so you can love others as God loves them.

Love Journey #29

Love me means getting away from the blind eyes that don't see.

I want to push and push, but if all you have for me is animosity, I can only pray for you and keep it moving!

Love you enough to stop allowing folks to tear you down when you're trying to bring them up.

EBONY N'TANTALA

Hebrews 13:6

So we can confidently say

"The Lord is my helper;

I will not fear;

What can man do to me?"

Chapter 30

Speak up so they can hear you in the Back

I remember growing up, we sang, "Sticks and stones may break my bones, but words can never hurt me." That's the biggest lie ever told! Words hurt; it sucks when they stay with you—sticking to you like glue, returning to remembrance at the most inopportune time. The enemy will make sure to return you to the time of your hurt and get you stuck in it. While you struggle haplessly through past hurts and pains, you forget what God has called you to do.

Though the words people throw at you may wound you, don't allow them to make you. Do not falter, and don't give in or give up. God's call over your life is not just for you; it's for those who will need the words you bring. Your purpose and assignment can NOT be derailed because of someone else's issues.

Take the issues they have about you and learn from them

or throw them away. But DON'T let them control your life or what God has for you to do. He never said everyone would agree with what He has given you; He just said DO.
IT'S your choice to do it or let it go.

You are valuable!
Know your worth!

Be about your Father's Business!

Journal Time

1. Have you allowed words to keep you stuck in your past hurts and pain?
2. If you haven't done so, write down all the hurt and pain and keep them on the page. Let the words rest on the page and not in your heart.

3. If you get stuck in your past, where is it, and why?

Love Journey #30

Loving you means not giving up on the call that's on your life.

Loving you means not throwing in the towel when it's handed to you.

Loving you means not allowing yourself to believe the lies spoken over your life.

Loving you means forgetting things that are past and

pressing towards the mark of God's high calling, regardless of what you are currently going through.

Let your love journey continue!

EBONY N'TANTALA

2 Corinthians 5:17

Therefore, if anyone is in Christ

he is a new creation.

The old has passed away;

behold, The new has come.

Chapter 31

FRESH START

When you feel you're fighting for your life, man or woman up, beat the hell out of the enemy, clean your scars, and move on. Don't wallow; God already has it rigged for you.

Loving yourself means not allowing someone else's negativity to change you.

YOU are the agent of change!

YOU change the temperature and the atmosphere to what it should be!

YOU love you enough to ignore

their foolishness and smile! Heap coals upon their heads!

Love yourself by kicking the negative people out of your life. If the people in your circle bring you down more than they lift you, get rid of them! You're worth more than that. Love you. You're worth it. You're valuable.

EBONY N'TANTALA

Journal Time

1. Do you find yourself just wanting to be with negative people? If yes, why?
2. Why do you feel you're not valuable enough to have people in your life who elevate you?
3. What are you going to do to change it?
4. Will you love yourself enough to remove those who don't value you?

Love Journey #31

Loving me is me knowing
I can make a fresh start
right here
right now.
I don't have to beg or grovel
I can ask God for it and have
faith to receive it
And a fresh start will begin.
I have to move into it
Flow in it, believe in it
and know that in it, God has
the victory in my life
I must allow my fresh start
to flow through me freely.

EBONY N'TANTALA

Chapter 32
What the Bible says love looks like

1 Corinthians 13(ESV)

If I speak in the tongues of men and of angels but have not love, I am a noisy gong or a clanging cymbal. 2 And if I have prophetic powers, and understand all mysteries and all knowledge, and if I have all faith, so as to remove mountains, but have not love, I am nothing. 3 If I give away all I have, and if I deliver up my body to be burned, [a] but have not love, I gain nothing.

4 Love is patient and kind; love does not envy or boast; it is not arrogant 5 or rude. It does not insist on its own way; it is not irritable or resentful; [b] 6 it does not rejoice at wrongdoing, but rejoices with the truth. 7 Love bears all things, believes all things, hopes all things, and endures all things.

8 Love never ends. As for prophecies, they will pass

away; as for tongues, they will cease; as for knowledge, it will pass away. 9 For we know in part and we prophesy in part, 10 but when the perfect comes, the partial will pass away. 11 When I was a child, I spoke like a child; I thought like a child, I reasoned like a child. When I became a man, I gave up childish ways. 12 For now we see in a mirror dimly, but then face to face. Now I know in part; then I shall know fully, even as I have been fully known.

13 So now faith, hope, and love abide, these three; but the greatest of these is love.

You must learn to love yourself first to give this type of love. I believe that God loves you more than you could ever fathom. My Friend Gabe Chen once told me, "God told me the universe cannot contain the love I have for you." Mind-blowing and eye-opening!!

This is the end of this journey, but not the end of

your journey. You are powerful by the blood of the Lamb, and you can be an agent of change and help those who are trying to change themselves. But first, you have to go on your love journey to assist them in theirs.

Loving you means enjoying being with just you.

And learning that other than Christ, you are your greatest asset! You need to believe in yourself and what God has put in you and trust The Holy Spirit to guide you.

Loving you means making you a priority! If you die or end up in the hospital, how will you help others? Don't let anyone silence your voice! Just know when to speak and when not to. When it's time to speak, speak with the boldness of The Holy Spirit!

Love Journey is a book that begins your self-discovery! Begin your love journey; discover your calling. Discover your purpose! Discover the love you have for yourself. There is something in you the world needs. Discover it and move in it. God gave it to you; ask Him what it is. Then move in it. People are waiting for you.

Allowing someone to see you walk through your trials helps others realize that all things are possible through Christ, who strengthens us.

Journal Time

1. What have you learned about yourself?
2. How are you going to start applying what you've learned?

Love, loving you, so you're able to love those around you

EBONY N'TANTALA

LOVE JOURNEY

www.ingramcontent.com/pod-product-compliance
Lightning Source LLC
Chambersburg PA
CBHW071447220526
45472CB00003B/705